CHRISTOPHER NORTON

microjazz

collection

1

Christopher Norton

To access audio, visit:
www.halleonard.com/mylibrary

Enter Code
3314-1498-3495-5676

Boosey & Hawkes Music Publishers Ltd
www.boosey.com

Published by Boosey & Hawkes Music Publishers Ltd
Aldwych House
71–91 Aldwych
London
WC2B 4HN

www.boosey.com

© Copyright 2011 by Boosey & Hawkes Music Publishers Ltd

ISMN 979-0-060-12251-4
ISBN 978-0-85162-618-5

Piano: Christopher Norton
Tracks: Frank Mizen
Audio Produced by Christopher Norton for CN Productions

Cover design by Design United Worldwide

www.christophernorton.com

Contents

microjazz collection 1

microjazz collection 1 contains the 24 pieces that were originally published as *microjazz for starters I* and *microjazz for starters II*, alongside four newer pieces which were added in 1997. Included for the first time with this edition is audio of brand-new backing and performance tracks, as well as useful teaching notes for each piece.

The pieces are printed in order of difficulty. Each technical and rhythmic feature encountered in a piece is dealt with, in order, in the preceding *microstudy*. These sets of simple exercises are designed to develop the technique and co-ordination necessary to play *microjazz*, and should be counted aloud wherever possible, particularly the tapped exercises, which can be practised with flat palms on knees, on the piano lid, or on any flat surface. It will help to start slowly, and only increase the speed once the co-ordination between right and left hands feels natural—then playing the piece should feel much easier.

The backing tracks highlight the range of styles encompassed by this book, and should be used to enthuse and inspire both your practice and performance. Moreover, the pieces in this collection are designed to be enjoyed and are meant to be performed in front of an audience—family, friends, other students, or whoever can be found!

This book forms part of a complete *microjazz* piano scheme which starts at the very first lesson with *microjazz for absolute beginners* (level 1) and progresses to *microjazz collection 3* (level 5).

Further supporting materials are available at www.christophernorton.com.

Christopher Norton, London, England, 2011

microjazz collection 1

microjazz collection 1 réunit l'ensemble des 24 morceaux déjà parus dans les recueils *microjazz for starters I* et *microjazz for starters II*, augmenté de quatre nouvelles pièces ajoutées en 1997. Cette édition comprend pour la première fois audio des enregistrements de nouvelles interprétations et d'accompagnements instrumentaux inédits, ainsi que des recommandations utiles à l'apprentissage de chacune des pièces.

Les pièces contenues dans *microjazz collection 1* sont présentés par ordre de difficulté, chacun étant précédé d'une *microstudy*, ou série d'exercices destinés à développer la technique et la coordination nécessaires à son exécution. Cette micro-étude aborde, dans l'ordre, toutes les difficultés techniques ou rythmiques soulevées par le morceau et il est recommandé de les jouer en comptant si possible à haute voix, notamment les exercices de rythmes frappés que l'on peut exécuter en tambourinant des mains sur les genoux, sur un couvercle de piano ou toute autre surface plane. Commencer, de préférence, lentement et n'accélérer que lorsque la coordination entre main droite et main gauche s'effectue naturellement – L'exécution du morceau s'en trouvera grandement facilitée.

Les accompagnements instrumentaux illustrent l'éventail des styles rencontrés dans ce recueil et stimuleront autant l'exercice que l'exécution en public, les pièces étant conçues à des fins récréatives et destinées à être jouées devant un auditoire – famille, amis, collègues étudiants ou autres!

Ce recueil fait partie de la méthode complète de piano *microjazz* en cinq niveaux, de *microjazz for absolute beginners* (niveau 1) pour les débutants à *microjazz collection 3* (niveau 5).

Des supports additionnels sont disponibles sur le site www.christophernorton.com.

Christopher Norton, London, England, 2011

microjazz collection 1

microjazz collection 1 enthält die 24 Stücke, die ursprünglich als *microjazz for starters I* und *microjazz for starters II* herausgegeben wurden und vier weitere Stücke, die 1997 hinzugefügt wurden. Zum ersten Mal wurde diese Ausgabe mit audio versehen, die brandneue Einspielungen mit kompletter Besetzung, sowie Playalongs zu allen Kompositionen enthält. Zusätzlich gibt es zu jedem Stück hilfreiche Lehranmerkungen.

In der *microjazz collection 1* wurden die Stücke in der Reihenfolge ihres Schwierigkeitsgrades angeordnet. Jedes Stück wird von einer *micro-studie* eingeleitet—einer Gruppe einfacher Übungen, die der Entwicklung der erforderlichen Spieltechnik und –koordination für *microjazz* dient. Jede technische und rhythmische Besonderheit, der man in einem Stück begegnet, wurde stufenweise in der vorangehenden *micro-studie* behandelt. Die *micro-studien* sollten—wenn möglich—laut mitgezählt werden, insbesondere die geklopften Übungen, die entweder mit flachen Händen auf den Knien bzw. dem Klavierdeckel oder einer beliebigen flachen Oberfläche geübt werden können. Am besten sollte man langsam anfangen und die Geschwindigkeit erst steigern, wenn die Koordination der linken und rechten Hand natürlich und selbstverständlich geworden ist—das Spielen des Stücks sollte danach sehr viel einfacher sein.

Die Begleiteinspielungen geben die stilistische Bandbreite wieder, die in diesem Band anzutreffen ist. Das Ziel hierbei ist es, den Enthusiasmus und die Inspiration für das Üben und Vortragen zu wecken. Die Stücke der *microjazz collection 1* sollen Freude bereiten und vor Publikum vorgetragen werden; im Kreis der Familie, vor Freunden, Mitschülern und allen anderen interessierten Zuhörern.

Dieses Buch ist Teil eines kompletten *microjazz*-Klavierprogramms, das mit der ersten Lektion in *microjazz for absolute beginners* (Stufe 1) beginnt und mit *microjazz collection 3* (Stufe 5) abschließt.

Weiteres Begleitmaterial finden Sie im Internet unter www.christophernorton.com.

Christopher Norton, London, England, 2011

Microstudies 1

Tap these rhythms. Count aloud at first.

Tapoter les rythmes. Compter tout haut pour commencer

Klopfen Sie diese Rhythmen. Zählen Sie zuerst laut.

それぞれのリズムをたたく。初めは声を出して数えながら。

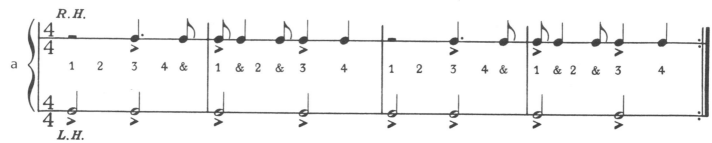

Left hand tapped, right hand on the keyboard.

Tapoter avec la main gauche; la main droite sur le clavier.

Linke Hand klopft, rechte Hand auf der Tastatur.

左手でリズム打ちをしながら右手は鍵盤上に。

Both hands on the keyboard.

Les deux mains sur le clavier.

Beide Hände auf der Tastatur.

両手を鍵盤上に。

Legato left hand.

Legato de la main gauche.

Linke Hand legato.

左手のレガード。

Tap these rhythms.

Tapoter les rythmes.

Klopfen Sie diese Rhythmen.

リズム打ち。

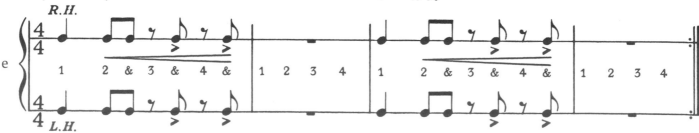

backing track – 01
full performance – 02

This piece contains a perky right-hand idea, repeated with variations. Each four-bar phrase should start *mf* and get quieter, with a dramatic *crescendo* to *ff* in the final bar. Strike all the accents firmly and follow the other articulation markings carefully.

1. Down to business

CHRISTOPHER NORTON

Microstudies 2

This exercise will help to strengthen the weaker fingers. Make sure each phrase is played smoothly.

Cet exercice aidera à fortifier les doigts les plus faibles. Veiller à ce que chaque phrase soit jouée de façon bien égale.

Mit dieser Übung stärken Sie Ihre schwächeren Finger. Achten Sie darauf, daß jede Phrase weich gespielt wird.

この練習は弱い指の強化に役立つ。各フレーズがスムースに弾けるように注意する。

a

Create a well-shaped phrase.

Créer une phrase bien formée.

Entwickeln Sie eine schöne Form der Phrase.

フレーズを明確に。

b

Two-note slurs.

Deux notes bien coulées.

Bindungen zwischen zwei Noten.

2音間のスラー。

c

Exaggerate the upward movement of the thumb.

Amplifier le mouvement du pouce vers le haut.

Betonen Sie die Aufwärtsbewegungen des Daumens.

親指を上げる動作を誇張する。

d

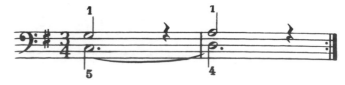

backing track – 03
full performance – 04

Start each phrase *mp* and *diminuendo* as marked. Create a sense of 'question' and 'answer' in the right-hand phrases, increasing the degree of expression throughout. Play the left hand *legato* and take your time at the end.

2. After the battle

CHRISTOPHER NORTON

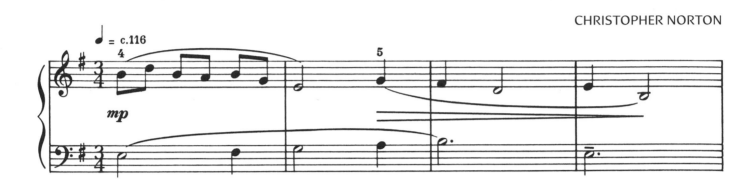

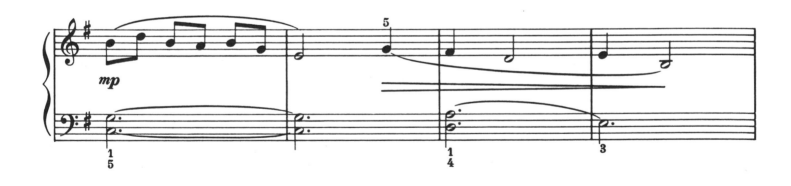

Microstudies 3

Make the left hand "sing".
Faire "chanter" la main gauche.

Lassen Sie die linke Hand "singen".
左手で歌う。

Tapped right hand, left hand on the keyboard.
Tapoter avec la main droite; la main gauche sur le clavier.

Rechte Hand klopft, linke Hand auf der Tastatur.
右手でリズム打ちをしながら左手は鍵盤上に。

Accent the 4th finger.
Accentuer avec l'auriculaire.

Akzent auf dem 4. Finger.
第4指のアクセント。

backing track – 05
full performance – 06

This is a swing piece so make sure there is a relaxed 'long–short' feel in the right-hand melody. Accent notes where marked, even if off the beat. Make sure there is complete silence between the right-hand phrases, but keep the left hand very smooth.

3. Struttin'

CHRISTOPHER NORTON

Microstudies 4

Tap with both hands and say the right-hand rhythm:
Taper le rythme des deux mains, en comptant à haute voix la main droite:

Klopfe mit beiden Händen und sprich den Rhythmus der rechten Hand mit:
両手パートをタップし、声を出して右手のリズムを歌います。

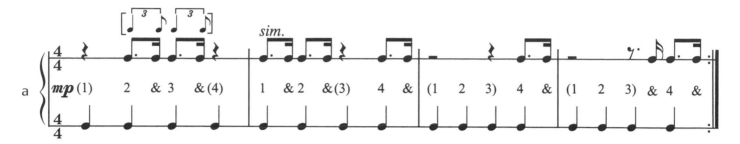

Right hand on the keyboard, left hand still tapped:
Main droite sur le clavier; la gauche continue à battre le rythme:

Rechte Hand auf den Tasten, linke Hand klopft weiter:
右手でピアノを弾きながら、左手はタップしてください。

Practise this change of hand position:
S'exercer au changement de position suivant:

Übe diesen Wechsel der Handposition:
この手のポジション変化を練習します。

The left hand changes position. Keep ♩ short!
La main gauche change le position. Éviter de faire durer le ♩!

Die linke Hand wechselt ihre Position. Halte ♩ kurz!
左手のポジションが変わります。♩を短く切ること！

Tap this rhythm until it feels comfortable:
Battre le rythme suivant jusqu'à ce que se fasse sans effort:

Klopfe diesen Rhythmus, bis Du Dich damit sicher fühlst:
気持ちよく続けられるようになるまで、このリズムをタップしてください。

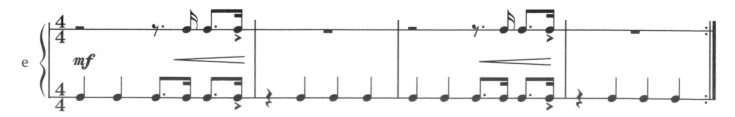

backing track – 07
full performance – 08

It's that 'long–short' swing pattern again! Make sure the left hand is not too loud and is always *staccato* (apart from at the very end). Slightly accent the first note of every right-hand phrase, and ensure the listener 'hears' every rest.

4. New confidence

CHRISTOPHER NORTON

Microstudies 5

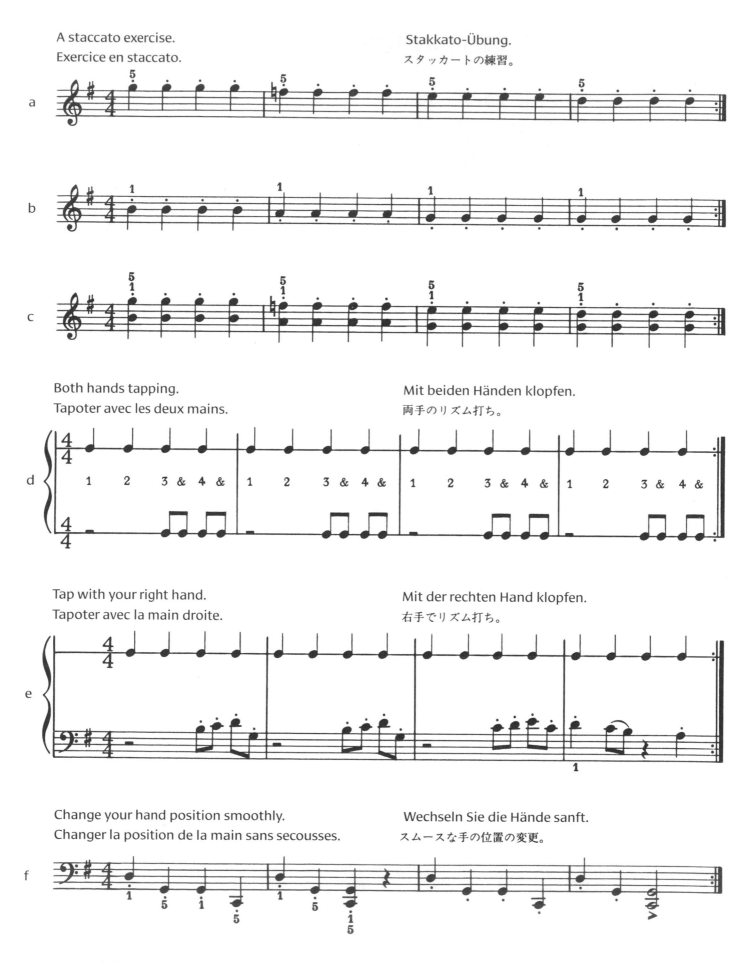

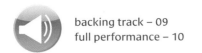

backing track – 09
full performance – 10

Make the top note of the right-hand chords sing out slightly more than the bottom note. Play with a relaxed wrist, with more weight from the arm added for the *crescendo* passages. Make sure the left-hand articulation is observed.

5. Tram stop

CHRISTOPHER NORTON

Microstudies 6

Count aloud and tap with your left hand.

Compter à haute voix et tapoter avec la main gauche.

Zählen Sie laut, und klopfen Sie mit der linken Hand.

声を出して数えながら左手でリズム打ち。

a

Count aloud and tap with your right hand.

Compter à haute voix et tapoter avec la main droite.

Zählen Sie laut, und klopfen Sie mit der rechten Hand.

声を出して数えながら右手でリズム打ち。

b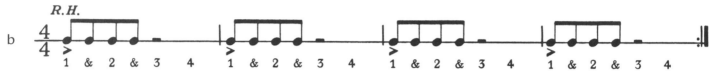

Count aloud and tap with both hands.

Compter à haute voix et tapoter des deux main.

Zählen Sie laut, und klopfen Sie mit beiden Händen.

声を出して数えながら両手でリズム打ち。

c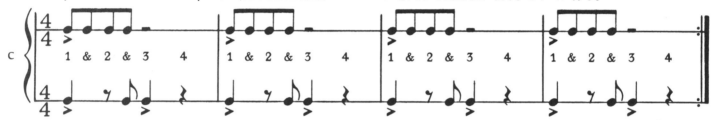

Left hand on the keyboard.

La main gauche sur le clavier.

Linke Hand auf der Tastatur.

左手は鍵盤上に。

d

Still counting aloud, play this on the keyboard.

Continuer à compter à haute voix et jouer cet air sur le clavier.

Immer noch laut zählen, und auf der Tastatur mitspielen.

声を出して数えながら弾く。

e

Practise slowly and legato.

Jouer lentement et legato.

Langsam und legato üben.

ゆっくり、そしてレガードで練習する。

f

backing track – 11
full performance – 12

Imagine the melody of this expressive country-style tune is being played by a fiddle player. Keep the dynamic of the left hand lower than the right hand throughout, and play the melody very *legato*.

6. Country ballad

CHRISTOPHER NORTON

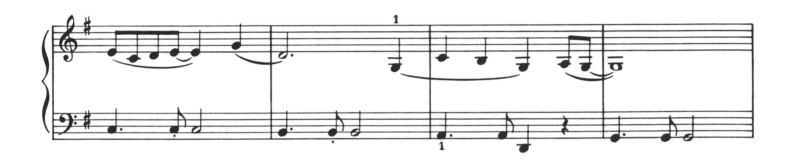

14

Microstudies 7

Keep the scale smooth by passing the thumb under.

Jouer les gammes legato en mettant le pouce endessous.

Achten Sie auf die Gleichmäßigkeit der Tonleitern, indem der Daumen untergesetzt wird.

親指をくぐらせながら音階をなめらかに弾く。

a

Accents on weaker fingers.

Accentuer avec les doigts les plus faibles.

Akzente mit den schwächeren Fingern.

弱い指でのアクセント。

b

Tap these rhythms and count aloud.

Tapoter ces rythmes en comptant à haute voix.

Klopfen Die diese Rhythmen und zählen Sie laut.

声を出して数えながらリズム打ち。

c

d

e

Count aloud and tap with both hands.

Compter à haute voix et tapoter des deux mains.

Zählen Sie laut, und klopfen Sie mit beiden Händen.

声を出して数えながら両手でリズム打ち。

f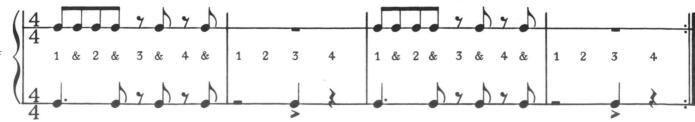

backing track – 13
full performance – 14

This piece contains some tricky rhythms, especially in bars 7 and 15, but the *microstudies* opposite will help you master these. Follow the articulation carefully to create a more interesting performance. How quietly can you play the final note?

7. Stairway

CHRISTOPHER NORTON

Microstudies 8

Practise these position changes. The fingering is important!

S'exercer au changement de position suivant. Le doigté est important!

Übe diese Positionswechsel. Der Fingersatz ist wichtig!

このポジション変化を練習します。指使いを必ず守ること！

Don't leave gaps between the notes, or play the thumb notes too heavily.

Ne pas introduire de séparation sonore entre les notes et ne pas appuyer trop fort avec le pouce.

Lasse keine Pausen zwischen den Noten; schlage die Daumennoten nicht zu stark an.

音符と音符の間に間をあけないこと。

親指の音だけが重くなりすぎないように注意。

Play the rhythm of the melody on one note. Count aloud:

Jouer le rythme de la mélodie sur une seule note. Compter à voix haute:

Spiele den Rhythmus der Melodie auf einer Note. Zähle laut mit:

ひとつの音だけを使って、メロディーのリズムを弾きます。声を出してカウントしましょう。

Practise legato pedalling, left hand only first:

S'exercer à utiliser la pédale pour obtenir un legato. Commencer par la main gauche seule:

Übe legato Pedalbedienung, zunächst nur mit der linken Hand:

ペダルを使ってレガートに弾く練習をします。まずは左手だけで。

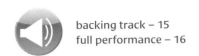

backing track – 15
full performance – 16

Use the sustain pedal to create warmth and colour, but ensure you still play the right-hand melody as *legato* as possible. Each phrase should be shaped expressively, and the grace notes conjure the image of snowflakes—light and unaccented.

8. Snow scene

CHRISTOPHER NORTON

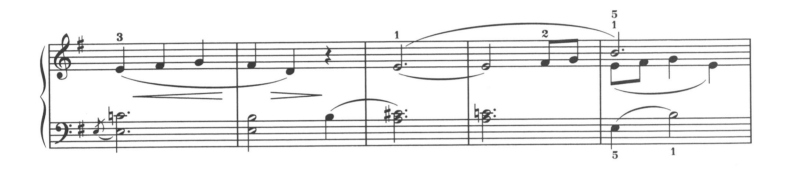

Microstudies 9

Make each phrase legato.
Jouer chaque phrase legato.

Spielen Sie jede Phrase legato.
それぞれのフレーズをレガードで。

Tap with your right hand.
Tapoter avec la main droite.

Klopfen Sie mit der rechten Hand.
右手でリズム打ち。

Play the same rhythm on one note.
Jouer le même rythme sur une seule note.

Spielen Sie denselben Rhythmus auf einer Note.
同一音による同一リズム型の演奏。

backing track – 17
full performance – 18

Fall gently with the left arm on the first and third beat of each bar, rising slightly through the wrist on the passing notes. Similarly, lift the right-hand wrist on the last note of each phrase to avoid a bump. The final chord should be a delicate *p*.

9. Cowboy song

CHRISTOPHER NORTON

Microstudies 10

backing track – 19
full performance – 20

Create a marked contrast between the light 'kick' given to the *staccato* notes and the weight of the accented notes in the main right-hand figure. Note the complete silence in the left hand on the third and fourth beats of several bars.

10. A day in Majorca

CHRISTOPHER NORTON

Microstudies 11

Legato between the hands.
Legato des deux mains.

Mit beiden Händen legato.
片方の手からもう片方の手へのレガード。

Tap with both hands.
Tapoter avec les deux mains.

Klopfen Sie mit beiden Händen.
両手でリズム打ち。

Hands together.
Les deux mains ensemble.

Beide Hände zusammen.
両手いっしょに。

backing track – 21
full performance – 22

Be bold and imaginative with your 'toy soldiers', using the dynamic and articulation markings to dramatic effect. Watch out for the changing time signatures.

11. Toy soldiers

CHRISTOPHER NORTON

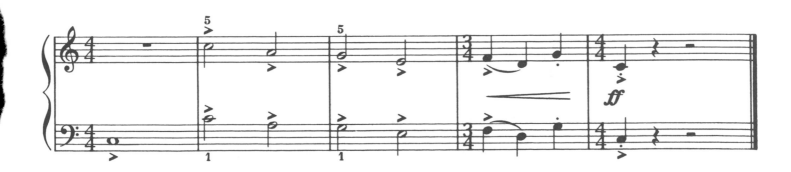

Microstudies 12

Practise this fingering:
S'exercer au doigté suivant:

Übe diesen Fingersatz:
この指使いを練習してください。

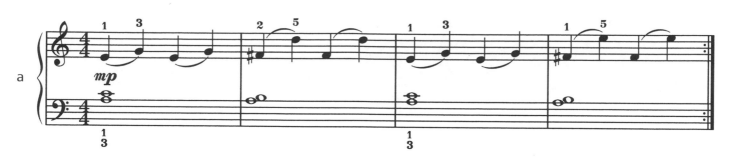

Smooth changes from one hand to the other:
Passage en douceur d'une main à l'autre:

Saubere Übergänge von einer Hand zur anderen:
片方の手から他の手への受け渡しをスムーズに。

Pass your thumb under smoothly:
Passer le pouce par dessous en douceur:

Führe Deinen Daumen sauber durch:
スムーズに親指をくぐらせます。

Get used to the position change:
Se familiariser avec le changement de position suivant:

Gewöhne Dich an den Positionswechsel:
ポジション変化に慣れてください。

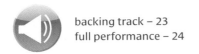

backing track – 23
full performance – 24

Don't rely on the pedal to achieve a *legato* line, and take extra care to achieve a smooth transition between the right and left hand in bar 4. Make the echo passage (*piu p*) an expressive highlight of the piece, even though it is quieter.

12. Questions

CHRISTOPHER NORTON

Microstudies 13

backing track – 25
full performance – 26

Use the weight of your arm to create the accents. Drop and rise with the wrist when you play two-note slurs. Create a dramatic contrast dynamically during the last four bars, ending with a 'cool' *p* chord.

13. On the right lines

CHRISTOPHER NORTON

Microstudies 14

backing track – 27
full performance – 28

Use the slurs to convey the easy-going feel of this piece, while carefully placing the accents and *staccato* to add a dash of extrovert flair. Observe the long wind-down from *f* to the soft, whimsical 'cha-cha-cha' ending.

14. Riviera

CHRISTOPHER NORTON

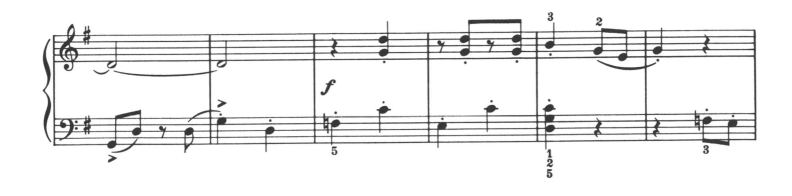

Microstudies 15

Count aloud.
Compter à haute voix.

Zählen Sie laut.
声を出して数える。

a

Tap with both hands. Count aloud.
Tapoter avec les deux mains. Compter à haute voix.

Klopfen Sie mit beiden Händen. Zählen Sie laut.
両手でリズム打ち。声を出して数える。

d
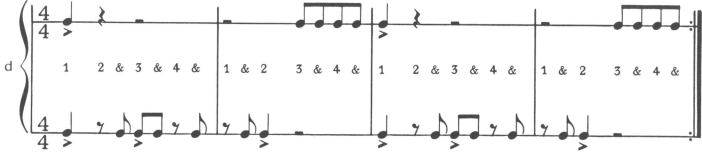

Play legato.
Jouer legato.

Spielen Sie legato.
レガートで弾く。

e

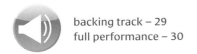

backing track – 29
full performance – 30

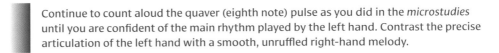

Continue to count aloud the quaver (eighth note) pulse as you did in the *microstudies* until you are confident of the main rhythm played by the left hand. Contrast the precise articulation of the left hand with a smooth, unruffled right-hand melody.

15. A thought

CHRISTOPHER NORTON

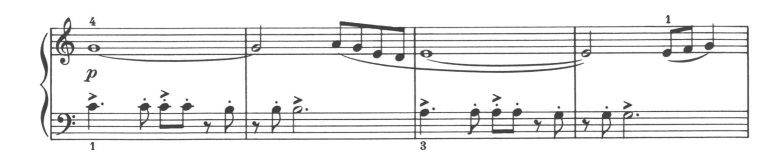

32

Microstudies 16

Tap this rhythm. Count the right hand out loud (bracketed numbers quieter!):

Battre le rythme, en comptant à haute voix la main droite (et en baissant la voix pour les chiffres entre parenthèses!):

Klopfe diesen Rhythmus. Zähle die rechte Hand laut mit (Nummern in Klammern leiser!):

このリズムをタップします。右手パートを声を出してカウントしてください（ただしカッコ内の番号は小さい声で！）

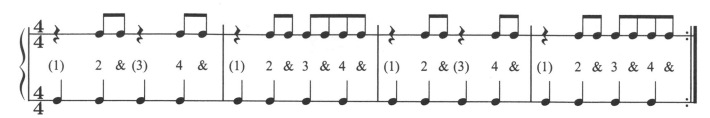

a

Make sure there's a space between the notes:

Attention à bien détacher les notes:

Achte darauf, zwischen den Noten Pausen zu lassen:

音符と音符の間に、間を置くこと。

b

Practise changing hand position:

S'exercer au changement de position suivant:

Übe das Wechseln der Handposition:

手のポジションを変える練習をします。

c

"Fall" on the right-hand notes marked ↓ :

↓ = drop wrist

↑ = lift wrist

——→ = a gradual rise of the wrist

Laisser tomber le poignet pour les notes de la main droite marquées ↓ :

↓ = laisser tomber le poignet

↑ = lever le poignet

——→ = lever progressivement le poignet

"Fall" auf den rechten Noten, die mit ↓ gekennzeichnet sind:

↓ = Handgelenk senken

↑ = Handgelenk anheben

——→ = langsames Heben des Handgelenks

右手パートの↓のついた音符の上に"落とし"ます。

↓ = 手首を落とす。

↑ = 手首を上げる。

→ = 手首を次第に引き上げていく。

d

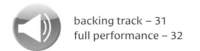

backing track – 31
full performance – 32

Practise the left hand separately at first, striving to achieve a light, *staccato* effect. Keep this accompanying line at a lower dynamic than the graceful right-hand melody, and don't let the piece become too loud at any point.

16. A short walk

CHRISTOPHER NORTON

Microstudies 17

Tap these rhythms. Count aloud at first.
Tapoter ces rythmes. Pour commencer compter à haute voix.

Klopfen Sie diese Rhythmen. Zählen Sie zuerst laut.
リズム打ちの練習。初めは声を出して数えながら。

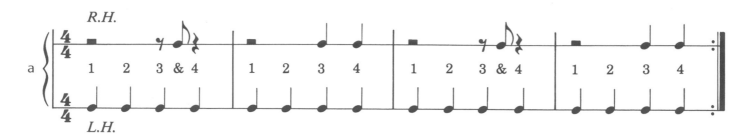

Left hand tapped, right hand on the keyboard.
Tapoter de la main gauche, main droite sur le clavier.

Linke Hand klopft, rechte Hand auf der Tastatur.
左手はリズム打ち、右手は鍵盤の上に。

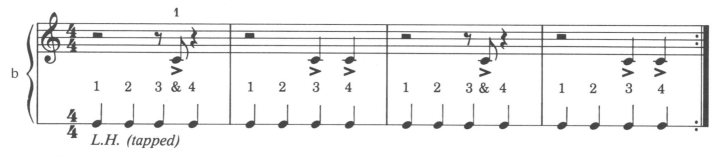

Both hands on the keyboard.
Les deux mains sur le clavier.

Beide Hände auf der Tastatur.
両手を鍵盤の上に。

Practise this fingering. Always staccato!
Pratiquer ce doigté. Toujours staccato!

Üben Sie diesen Fingersatz. Immer staccato!
指使いの練習。常にスタッカートで。

Hands together.
Des deux mains.

Beide Hände zusammen.
両手で。

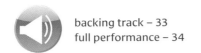

backing track – 33
full performance – 34

This piece has a rock feel, so exaggerate the dynamics and give the accents some bite!
Keep the left-hand notes short and bouncy, and drop the weight of the arm on the last note
of the piece.

17. Sprightly

CHRISTOPHER NORTON

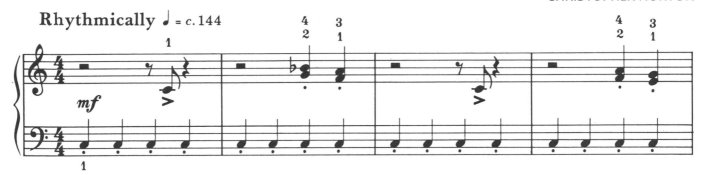

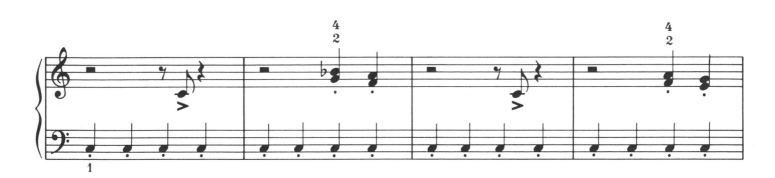

Microstudies 18

Tap this rhythm. Count aloud at first.

Tapoter ce rythme. Commencer par compter à haute voix.

Klopfen Sie diese Rhythmen. Zählen Sie zuerst laut.

リズム打ちの練習。初めは声を出して数えながら。

Left hand tapped, right hand on the keyboard.

Tapoter de la main gauche, main droite sur le clavier.

Linke Hand klopft, rechte Hand auf der Tastatur.

左手はリズム打ち、右手は鍵盤の上に。

Make sure the notes sound together.

S'assurer que les notes sont à l'unisson.

Achten Sie darauf, daß die Noten gut zusammen klingen.

和音が同時に出るように気を付けること。

Both hands on the keyboard.

Les deux mains sur le clavier.

Beide Hände auf der Tastatur.

両手を鍵盤の上に。

Change hand position smoothly.

Changez en douceur la position de la main.

Wechseln Sie die Hände sanft.

手の位置をスムーズに変えること。

Staccato left hand.

Main gauche staccato.

Linke Hand staccato.

左手でスタッカート。

backing track – 35
full performance – 36

Create a crisp, wintry atmosphere by playing the opening chords softly and lightly. Lift the hand gracefully to shape the *legato* phrases. Use the *rit.* at the end of the piece to see how quietly, yet precisely, you can play the final chord.

18. A winter song

CHRISTOPHER NORTON

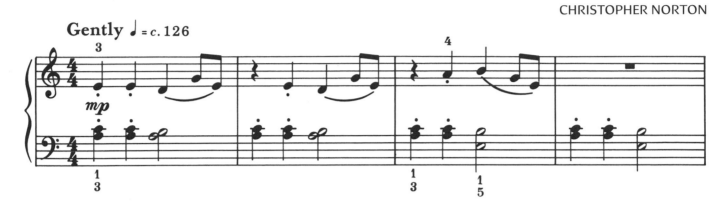

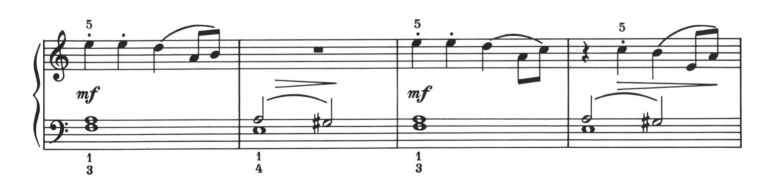

Microstudies 19

A staccato left hand.

Main gauche staccato.

Linke Hand staccato.

左手でスタッカート。

Tapped right hand, left hand on the keyboard.
Count aloud at first.

Tapoter de la main droite, main gauche sur le clavier.
Commencer par compter à haute voix.

Rechte Hand klopft, linke Hand auf der Tastatur.
Zählen Sie zuerst laut.

右手はリズム打ち、左手は鍵盤の上に。
初めは声を出して数えながら。

Practise this fingering.

Pratiquer ce doigté.

Üben Sie diesen Fingersatz.

指使いの練習。

Practise this fingering.

Pratiquer ce doigté.

Üben Sie diesen Fingersatz.

指使いの練習。

Count aloud.

Compter à haute voix.

Zählen Sie laut.

声を出して数えながら。

backing track – 37
full performance – 38

This is another swing piece, so play the dotted figures with a relaxed triplet feel. Embrace the small *crescendos* that lead into the downbeat accents, while keeping the left hand light and airy throughout—*mp* to the right hand's *mf*.

19. Tut-tuttin'

CHRISTOPHER NORTON

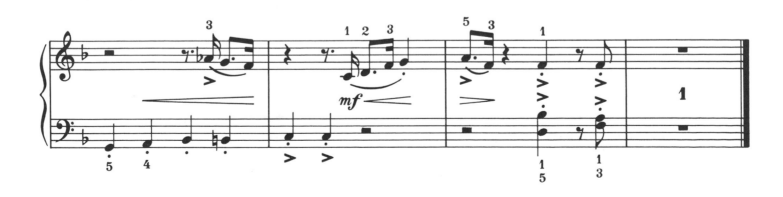

Microstudies 20

A scale of G major. Count aloud at first.

Gamme en sol majeur. Commencer par compter à haute voix.

Eine G-Dur-Tonleiter. Zählen Sie zuerst laut.

ト長調。初めは声を出して数えながら。

Another scale of G major.

Une autre gamme en sol majeur.

Noch eine G-Dur-Tonleiter.

ト長調。

Hands together.

Des deux mains.

Beide Hände zusammen.

両手で。

Play smoothly. Count aloud at first.

Jouer en douceur. Commencer par compter à haute voix.

Spielen Sie sanft. Zählen Sie zuerst laut.

スムーズに演奏すること。初めは声を出して数えながら。

A change of finger on one note.

Changer de doigt sur une note.

Fingerwechsel auf einer Note.

一つの音符上の指の交換。

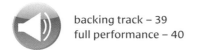

backing track – 39
full performance – 40

Give the right-hand melody an elegant shape by observing the marked *crescendos* and *diminuendos*. Let the left hand take the lead into bar 8, accompanied by a crisp rhythm in the right hand. Aim for absolute togetherness.

20. Walking together

CHRISTOPHER NORTON

Microstudies 21

Tap these rhythms. Count aloud at first.

Tapoter ces rythmes. Commencer par compter à haute voix.

Klopfen Sie diese Rhythmen. Zählen Sie zuerst laut.

リズム打ちの練習。初めは声を出して数えながら。

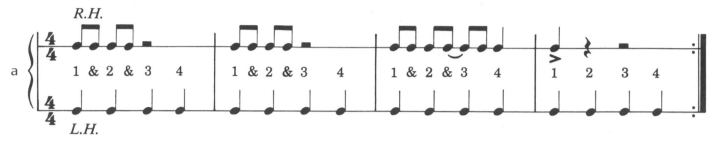

Right hand tapped, left hand on the keyboard.

Tapoter de la main droite, main gauche sur le clavier.

Rechte Hand klopft, linke Hand auf der Tastatur.

右手はリズム打ち、左手は鍵盤の上に。

Staccato left hand.

Main gauche staccato.

Linke Hand staccato.

左手でスタッカート。

Give the rests full value. Count aloud at first.

Donner à la pause toute sa valeur. Commencer par compter à haute voix.

Halten Sie die Pausen sorgfältig ein. Zählen Sie zuerst laut.

休止符は完全に休むこと。初めは声を出して数えながら。

Hands together. Keep the left hand staccato.

Des deux mains. Poursuivre le staccato de la main gauche.

Beide Hände zusammen. Die linke Hand spielt weiter staccato.

両手で。左手はスタッカート。

backing track – 41
full performance – 42

It may seem tricky at first, but try to play the left hand *staccato* where marked, even though the right hand has slurred figures. Gracefully lift the right-hand wrist on the last note of each *legato* phrase, and ensure the note doesn't extend into the rest.

21. Rag time

CHRISTOPHER NORTON

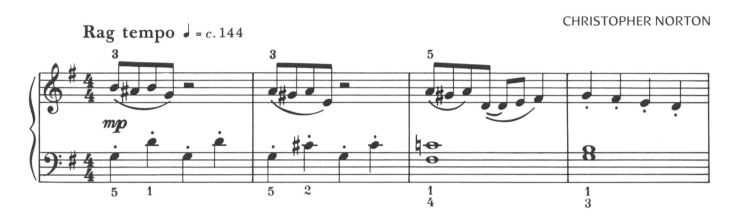

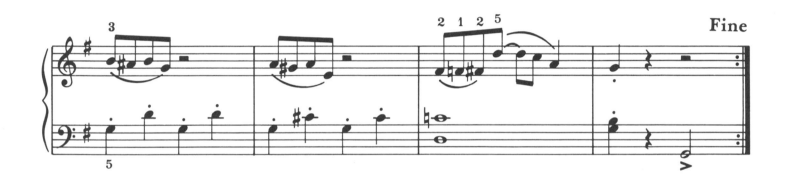

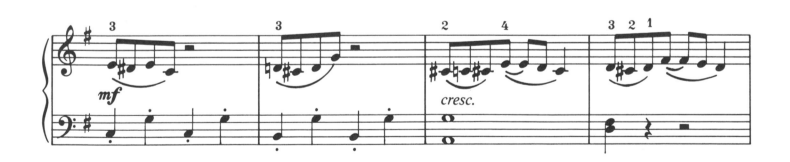

Microstudies 22

Play legato.
Jouer legato.

Spielen Sie legato.
レガートで。

Practise this pedalling.
Pratiquer ce jeu des pédales.

Üben Sie diese Pedalisierung.
ペダル使いの練習。

Hands together.
Des deux mains.

Beide Hände zusammen.
両手で。

Change smoothly.
Changement en douceur.

Sanfter Wechsel der Hände.
スムーズに変えること。

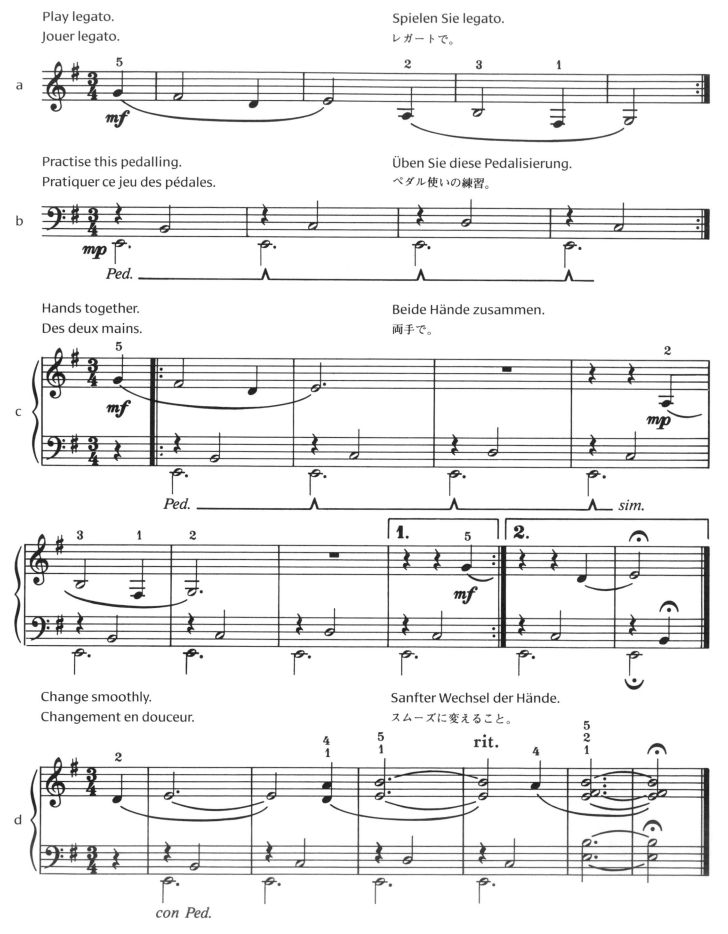

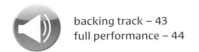

backing track – 43
full performance – 44

Practise the left hand by itself, concentrating on the pedalling to ensure the joins are seamless. Then practise the right hand without the pedal, still aiming to create a smooth line. Notice the 'question and answer' effect in the right hand.

22. Duet for one

CHRISTOPHER NORTON

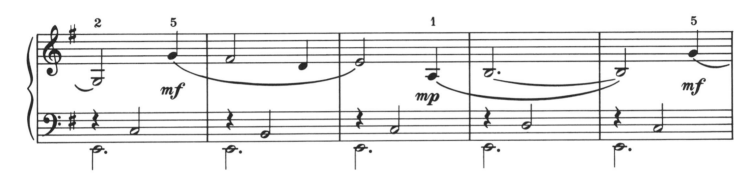

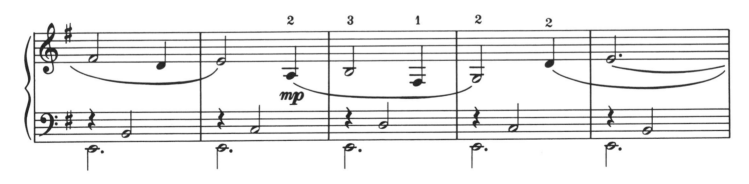

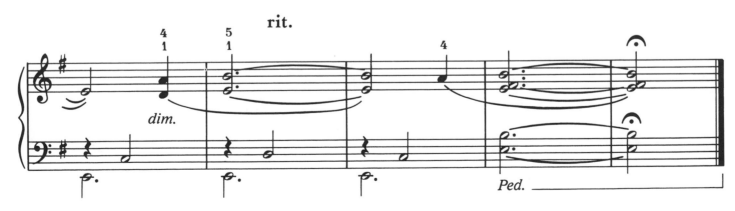

Microstudies 23

Change fingers smoothly.
Changer de doigts en douceur.

Wechseln Sie die Finger sanft.
指をスムーズに変えること。

Count aloud at first.
Commencer par compter à haute voix.

Zählen Sie zuerst laut.
初めは声を出して数えながら。

Change smoothly.
Changement en douceur.

Sanfter Wechsel.
スムーズに変えること。

Hands together.
Des deux mains.

Beide Hände zusammen.
両手で。

rit.

backing track – 45
full performance – 46

Drop slightly on the first note of each bar in your left hand, creating a small arc as you move smoothly to the next note. Play the right hand *legato* without any bumps on notes played by the thumb.

23. Lonesome trail

CHRISTOPHER NORTON

Thoughtfully ♩ = c.126

Microstudies 24

Play smoothly.
Jouer en douceur.

Spielen Sie sanft.
スムーズに演奏すること。

Tap these rhythms.
Tapoter ces rythmes.

Klopfen Sie diese Rhythmen.
リズム打ちの練習。

Right hand tapped, left hand on the keyboard.
Tapoter de la main droite, main gauche sur le clavier.

Rechte Hand klopft, linke Hand auf der Tastatur.
右手はリズム打ち、左手は鍵盤の上に。

Practise this fingering.
Pratiquer ce doigté.

Üben Sie diesen Fingersatz.
指使いの練習。

Take over smoothly.
Reprise en douceur.

Sanfter Wechsel der Hände.
スムーズに引き継ぐこと。

backing track – 47
full performance – 48

This is another relaxed swing piece. Keep the *staccato* notes light and drop with some arm weight on the accents. Be scrupulous in your following of the articulation in both hands, and ensure complete silence where rests are indicated.

24. Ambling

CHRISTOPHER NORTON

Microstudies 25

Tap these rhythms. Count aloud at first.
Tapoter ces rythmes. Commencer par compter à haute voix.

Klopfen Sie diese Rhythmen. Zählen Sie zuerst laut.
リズム打ちの練習。初めは声を出して数えながら。

Tap again.
Tapoter encore.

Nochmals klopfen.
リズム打ちの練習。

Left hand staccato.
Main gauche staccato.

Linke Hand staccato.
左手でスタッカート。

Right hand on the keyboard, left hand tapped.
Main droite sur le clavier, la main gauche tapoté.

Rechte Hand auf der Tastatur, linke Hand klopft.
右手は鍵盤の上に、左手はリズム打ち。

Crossed hands.
Mains croisés.

Hände gekreuzt.
手を交差させて。

backing track – 49
full performance – 50

Don't be tempted to take this piece too fast as there are semiquavers (16th notes) to fit in. Drop with the weight of the arm on accents of any kind. Give the *f* a satisfyingly full-blooded sound, but remember to drop back to *mf* four bars later.

25. Cross-over

CHRISTOPHER NORTON

Steady ♩ = c. 86

Microstudies 26

Tap these rhythms.
Tapoter ces rythmes.

Klopfen Sie diese Rhythmen.
リズム打ちの練習。

Practise this fingering.
Pratiquer ce doigté.

Üben Sie diesen Fingersatz.
指使いの練習。

Tapped left hand, right hand on the keyboard.
Tapoter de la main gauche. Main droite sur le clavier.

Linke Hand klopft, rechte Hande auf der Tastatur.
左手はリズム打ち、右手は鍵盤の上に。

Staccato.
Staccato.

Staccato.
スタッカート。

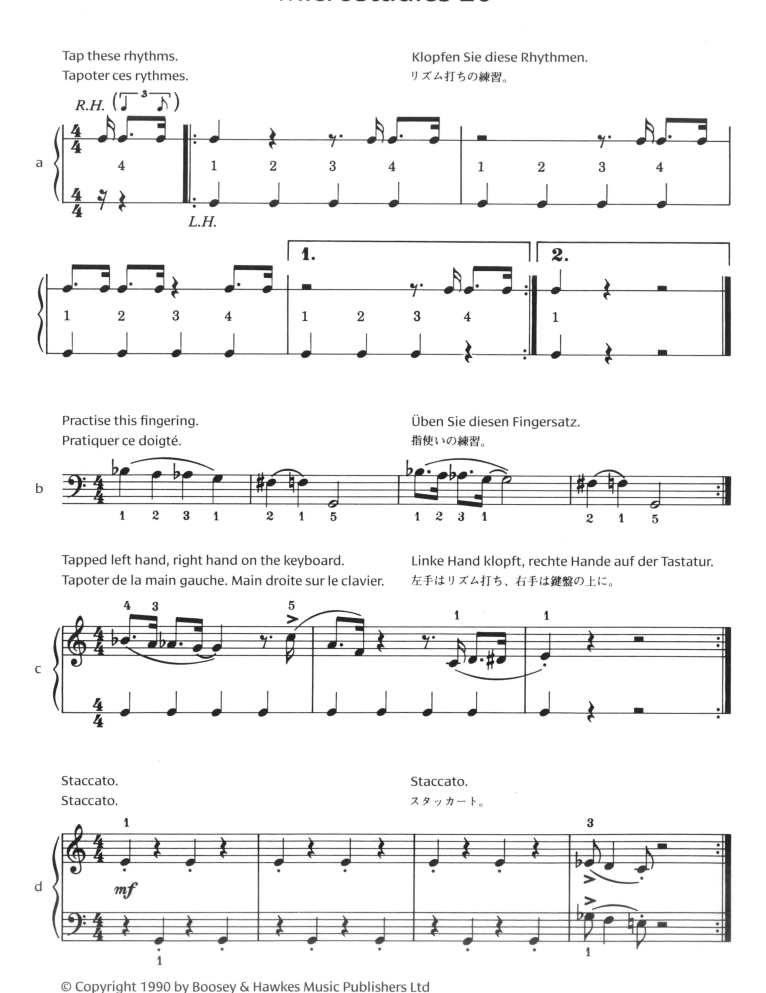

backing track – 51
full performance – 52

Imagine a clarinet and trombone playing this mellow swing piece as a dejected duet. Follow the helpful fingering indications. What can you do differently on the repeat?

26. A doleful song

CHRISTOPHER NORTON

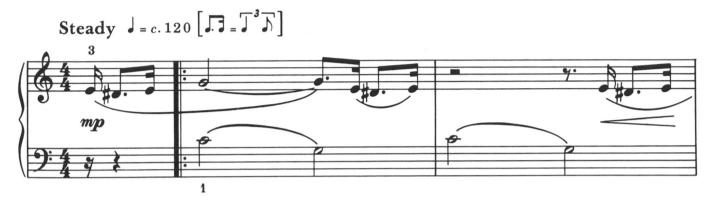

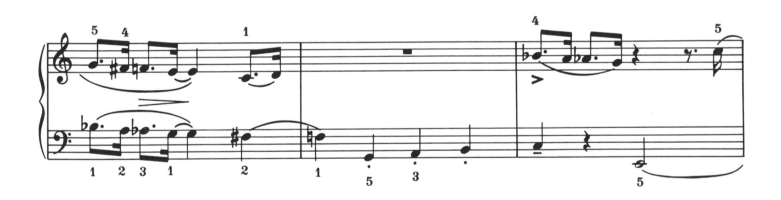

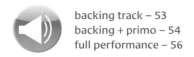

backing track – 53
backing + primo – 54
full performance – 56

Play quietly and smoothly, using the pedal to create a warm, sustained sound.
Start softly and never get too loud. Keep to a steady tempo.

27. Exotic travels

CHRISTOPHER NORTON

Secondo

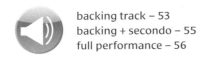

backing track – 53
backing + secondo – 55
full performance – 56

Play the semiquaver (16th note) passing notes more quietly than the main notes without rushing through them. Strive to create smooth melodic lines in both the right and left hands.

27. Exotic travels

CHRISTOPHER NORTON

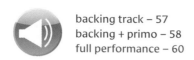

backing track – 57
backing + primo – 58
full performance – 60

Rests matter, especially when there are two people at the piano. Use a slight drop of the wrist to create the *tenuto* effect, but don't let the repeated notes get too heavy.

28. Tip top

CHRISTOPHER NORTON

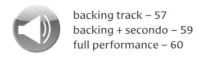

backing track – 57
backing + secondo – 59
full performance – 60

The right and left hands should be perfectly matched in terms of the articulation, dynamic and length of each note. The *p* ending should have a humorous effect—who can play quietest?

28. Tip top

CHRISTOPHER NORTON

Online Audio Tracklisting

Tracks 54/58 – backing track with primo piano part.
Tracks 55/59 – backing track with secondo piano part.